The Life and Times of

CLARA
BARTON

Mitchell Lane
PUBLISHERS

P.O. Box 196 · Hockessin, Delaware 19707

Titles in the Series

The Life and Times of

Abigail Adams
Alexander Hamilton
Benjamin Franklin
Betsy Ross
The Brothers Custer: Galloping to Glory
Clara Barton
Eli Whitney
Father Jacques Marquette
George Rogers Clark
Hernando Cortés
James Madison
John Adams
John Cabot
John Hancock
John Paul Jones
John Peter Zenger
Nathan Hale
Patrick Henry
Paul Revere
Peter Stuyvesant
Rosa Parks
Samuel Adams
Sir Walter Raleigh
Stephen F. Austin
Susan B. Anthony
Thomas Jefferson
William Penn

Profiles in American History

The Life and Times of

CLARA BARTON

Susan Sales Harkins and
William H. Harkins

Printing   1   2   3   4   5   6   7   8   9

Library of Congress Cataloging-in-Publication Data

Harkins, Susan Sales.
  The life and times of Clara Barton / by Susan Sales Harkins and William H. Harkins.
      p. cm.—(Profiles in American history)
  Includes bibliographical references and index.
  ISBN 978-1-58415-667-3 (library bound)
  1. Barton, Clara, 1821–1912. 2. American Red Cross—Biography—Juvenile literature.
  3. Nurses—United States—Biography—Juvenile literature. I. Harkins, William H.
  II. Title.
  HV569.B3H37 2009
  361.7'634092—dc22
  [B]
                                                                                2008008031

ABOUT THE AUTHORS: Susan and William Harkins live in Kentucky, where they enjoy writing together for children. Susan has written many books for adults and children. William is a history buff. In addition to writing, he is a member of the Air National Guard. They have written over a dozen titles for Mitchell Lane Publishers.

PHOTO CREDITS: Cover, pp. 1, 3, 6, 12, 18, 34, 39, 42—Library of Congress; p. 26—North Wind Picture Archives.

PUBLISHER'S NOTE: This story is based on the authors' extensive research, which they believe to be accurate. Documentation of such research is contained on page 46.
     The internet sites referenced herein were active as of the publication date. Due to the fleeting nature of some web sites, we cannot guarantee they will all be active when you are reading this book.
                                                                                PLB

Profiles in American History

Contents

*For Your Information

Clara Barton was a small child and a petite woman, but size was not an obstacle. She was a hard worker and never shirked her responsibilities.

CHAPTER 1

Angel of the Battlefield

Clara Barton found the stench and the mosquitoes at Armory Square Hospital almost unbearable. She could do nothing about the foul smell, but she could swat the flying insects. The severely wounded didn't even notice Clara's attempts to shoo the insects away. The bloodsuckers tormented the luckier ones—those well enough to feel their stings.

Clara spent most of her waking hours at the hospital. Today she had taken a comb to Sergeant Field of the Massachusetts Twenty-first.[1] He hadn't asked for much, just a comb. After cheating death on the battlefield, perhaps neat hair lent a sense of normalcy. It would be a long time before "her boys"[2] in Armory returned to their normal lives. Some never would.

On the way home that Saturday evening, Clara joined a crowd gathering at the wharf. Silently they watched battered troops cross the bridge over the Potomac River. The news spread quickly through the crowd—the second battle of Bull Run was over (August 28–30, 1862).

Clara wasted no time. Within hours she sat in a boxcar headed for the battlefield. Around ten o'clock the next morning, the train stopped. Soon the cargo doors opened onto a hazy drizzle.[3] Without pause, she lifted her skirt and jumped to the ground. She didn't have time to wait for a man to help her down, as a proper lady should. In a war, there was no time for social conventions. The wounded didn't

care about her ankles and petticoats. They were in pain. Mostly, she knew, they feared dying alone.

In every direction, Clara saw smoke from the battle's dying fires. At her feet lay the battle's wounded. Through the smoke drifted the moans and cries for water, home, mother, sweetheart. . . . Fairfax Station smelled of smoke, blood, and death. If she faltered now, the sorrow of it would eat her alive. She went to work instead.

Clara gathered every cooking tool she could find. When she was done, she had two water buckets, five tin cups, one camp kettle, one stew pan, two lanterns, four bread knives, and three plates.[4] With these simple tools, she would feed three thousand wounded men.

Clara gathered wood and built a huge fire. Fifteen minutes after jumping off the train, she was cooking food and bandaging wounds.[5]

Feeding the men was easier than Clara had first thought. There were boxes and boxes of canned foods. She cooked the contents and refilled the empty jars with warm soup, coffee, and water.

With just two lanterns, Clara and a few workers tended the three thousand wounded soldiers throughout the night. Whispering comforting words, she gave them water and treated their wounds.

Clara and the workers spent that night covering the men in blankets and quilts that northern women had donated to Clara's cause. When they ran out of blankets, they piled hay over the shivering men,[6] who lay so close that it was hard to walk between them. Just having the "angel of the battlefield" nearby seemed to calm them.[7]

On Monday morning, September 1, they spotted Confederate cavalry. Immediately, Union workers began to evacuate the wounded by train, but more wounded were still arriving. Clara refused to leave even one wounded soldier behind.

Around six o'clock a hard rain and artillery fire forced Clara to seek shelter in her tent. Through the tent's opening she watched the Twenty-first Massachusetts Regiment hold back the enemy.

Tuesday morning Clara worked fast to evacuate the remaining wounded before the Confederates reached them. She watched from the last train as Confederates set fire to Fairfax Station.

Back at home she slept for twenty-four hours, but she barely had time to regain her strength. The battle of Chantilly came fast on the heels of Bull Run. It was a devastating loss for the Union. Major General John Pope retreated to Washington, D.C., leaving no army between the citizens of Washington and the Confederates. Fortunately

The courageous General Phil Kearny was killed at the battle of Chantilly when he rode too close to Confederate lines.

the Confederates were too tired to chase Pope into Washington. Instead, they fell back and regrouped.

A few days later Clara was working quietly among the wounded left behind after the battle of Chantilly (September 1, 1862). Some were little more than boys. One lay bare-chested on the ground. When she reached down to wrap his torn shirt around his chest, the boy threw an arm around her neck and began to cry. "Don't you remember me?" he asked. "I am Charley Hamilton who used to carry your satchel home from school!"[8] Her teaching days seemed far away at that moment. On the battlefields of the Civil War, Clara met many of her former pupils.

That night Clara followed a doctor up the hill to help tend to the wounded. One young soldier was crying pitifully for his sister. Clara motioned for the men standing nearby to remove their lanterns. In the darkness, she knelt by the dying boy and took his hand. "Brother," she said. She kissed his forehead and laid her cheek against his. "Oh, Mary! Mary! You have come?"[9] Clara wrapped the dying soldier in blankets and placed his head on her lap. She sat with him until morning.

In the dawn light the young man saw that Clara wasn't his sister Mary. He begged Clara to get him back to Washington. His mother would find him there and bury him properly. If they left him in the Virginia woods, his mother would never find his body. It would probably be buried in a mass grave. It took a while, but Clara persuaded the surgeon to put Hugh Johnson on a train for Washington.

On Monday morning, wagons brought more wounded than the trains could evacuate. Many of the wounded had gone without food

or care for three days. Clara knew that they would be on the train for at least another twenty-four hours. She insisted that they feed the men before putting them on the trains.

That day Clara supervised as eight men loaded the wounded onto trains, built fires, cooked, fed the wounded, dug graves, and buried the dead. The last of the wounded were gone by three o'clock that afternoon, and not a minute too soon. The enemy was just over the hill.

A little later lightning lit the sky. The air was thick with the coming rain. Clara sat down to eat for the first time in two days. *Boom!* The ground shook from exploding artillery. The battle of Chantilly wasn't over. Lightning and artillery blasts lit the scarred battlefield and the wagons carrying more wounded.

Clara fed them what was left of the food. She beat crackers into crumbs and mixed them with wine, whiskey, water, and brown sugar. The wounded ate the gruel without complaint. When the last train pulled out, Clara climbed the small hill to her tent. She was weary and could barely put one foot in front of the other. She fell on the slippery hillside. Finally, she reached her tent and opened the flap to find the ground awash with rain. For two hours, she slept sitting up in her drenched tent.

At midnight the noise of a rumbling wagon woke Clara. Dripping wet, covered with grass and leaves, she left the tent and followed the wagon to tend to its wounded. Soon, she heard a single pipe and a muffled drum sound the retreat. All that day the wounded rolled in and the troops moved out. The enemy crashed through the wooded hills.

The next afternoon, an officer galloped up to Clara and warned her to leave that moment or risk capture. The last of the wounded were on the train, so Clara willingly left. As the train pulled out, she watched rebels set the station ablaze. Her train arrived in Washington around midnight. Clara had slept just two hours over the last four days.

Friday morning she checked patients at Armory Square Hospital. She found the name Hugh Johnson on the list of the dead. Chaplain Jackson pointed toward a nearby wagon and a coffin. Beside the coffin stood two women, Hugh's mother and his sister, Mary. Clara watched from a distance as Hugh's family prepared to take him home, as the dying soldier had requested.[10]

Armory Square Hospital

Ward K of the Amory Square Hospital

During the first few months of the Civil War, the army cared for its wounded in federal buildings, churches, and large houses. At one point, there were almost as many patients in Washington, D.C., as there were civilians. At the peak of the war, the Washington area had as many as eighty-five make-shift hospitals.

One of the largest Civil War hospitals was the Armory Square Hospital on the National Mall, built in the summer of 1862. It was a huge complex with one thousand beds in small buildings and tents. The smell was bad, but that wasn't a product of the hospital. The hospital was across from a canal, which was little more than an open sewer.

The site was close to major thoroughfares and was easily accessible to the wharves and railroad station. The wounded made their way from the battlefield to the wharves and depot. From there they traveled to the hospitals about town. The Armory Square Hospital was the hospital that Clara Barton frequented the most when she was in Washington.

The hospital's main building housed personnel and offices. There was a reception room, a dispensary, a linen room, a post office, a kitchen, a laundry, and a dining hall. Ten additional buildings served as wards for the patients. These buildings were 149 feet by 25 feet. Each held fifty beds.

Despite the high number of casualties, disease was the biggest killer. Typhoid and cholera killed twice as many soldiers as battle wounds.

After the war, the buildings were used for storage, and at one time they housed the United States Fish Commission. In January 1964, the hospital was demolished to make room for the Smithsonian's National Air and Space Museum.

For Your Information

11

Clara Barton, painted during the Civil War. As a child, Clara learned about armies and war from her father, Captain Stephen Barton.

CHAPTER
2

From Tot to Teacher

David Barton sprinted home over the ice and snow. His strict school held classes even on Christmas Day. Near home a neighbor called out to him to hurry, as there was a little tot waiting at home.[1] The baby had come! He dashed up the icy hill toward home. The small white farmhouse looked warm and cozy after his cold walk.

He found his brother and sisters standing just inside his parents' room. Clarissa Harlowe Barton seemed like a huge name for the tiny baby lying in the cradle his father had made.[2] He remembered the neighbor's call to him and dubbed her "Tot."[3] The family agreed that Tot was the best Christmas present they received in the year 1821.

Tot's siblings doted on her. Dorothea, the oldest, was seventeen. Her brothers, David and Stephen, were fifteen and thirteen. The youngest was Sally. She was almost eleven.

Eventually Tot grew into the name Clara. Growing up as the fifth child in a family full of mostly grown children was a challenge. As she grew, she had no playmates and was often lonely.[4]

Both older sisters taught Clara at home from an early age. By three she could read. They sent her to school at just four. In later years Clara said of her home schooling, "I have no knowledge of ever learning to read, or of a time that I did not do my own story reading."[5]

David taught her how to ride horses and play boys' games. In later years, she wrote about David's riding lessons: "It was his delight

to take me, a little girl of five years old, to the field, seize a couple of those beautiful young creatures . . . and gathering the reins of both bridles firmly in hand, throw me upon the back of one colt, spring upon the other himself, and catching me by one foot, and bidding me 'cling fast to the mane,' gallop away over field and fen. . . . Sometimes in later years, when I found myself suddenly on a strange horse in a trooper's saddle, flying for life or liberty in front of pursuit, I blessed the baby lessons of the wild gallops among the beautiful colts."[6]

Her older and accomplished siblings and her quick-tempered mother overwhelmed young Clara. Sarah Stone Barton was a strict and demanding mother. She swore when she was angry, and she was angry often. She once dismantled a new iron stove and threw it piece by piece into a pond because she didn't like it.[7]

Captain Stephen Barton was a hard worker with influence in the community. He often moderated town meetings. As a young man, he fought with General Wayne, also known as "Mad Anthony," during the Indian Wars.

Perhaps Clara inherited her disposition from her gentle father. Besides David, Captain Barton was Clara's best playmate as a small child. He told her stories of his years in the army. Later she wrote about the time he spent with her. "I listened breathlessly to his war stories. Illustrations were called for and we made battles and fought them. . . . Colonels, captains, and sergeants were given their proper place and rank. So with the political world; the President, Cabinet, and leading officers of the government were learned by heart."[8]

Her sisters took over the community's one-room school, and Clara studied under them until she was eight. She was sensitive and shy, which hindered her progress at school. At home, she learned quickly, but she was too shy to speak up for herself. She wouldn't ask for new clothes as she outgrew her things. Nor would she ask for new gloves when hers became worn.[9]

As an adult Clara said she remembered only fear as a small child.[10] "I had no playmates, but in effect six fathers and mothers. They were a family of school-teachers. All took charge of me, all educated me, each according to personal taste."[11] Her biographer, William E. Barton, contradicts this statement: " . . . her childhood memories were happy ones, and her affection for every member of the household was sincere and almost unbounded."[12] It's possible that

both statements are true. She was shy and introverted. Her parents and siblings had strong personalities and were successful. It's easy to understand how a child surrounded by so many accomplished and outspoken people would be fearful and yet happy at the same time.

Having a mentally ill older sister probably didn't help Clara's sensitive nature. Dorothea, who was called Dolly, had a mental breakdown when she was twenty-three and Clara was just six. There was no treatment or help for the mentally ill. Eventually Dolly became violent. She once tried to kill her sister-in-law with an ax. Despite the iron bars on her windows and the lock on her door, she escaped the Barton house at least twice. Dolly was mentally ill until her death in 1842.

Clara was seven or eight when her family moved to a new farm. Her older siblings remained at the old farm. She was away from Dolly's ravings, and she finally had playmates her own age. Her cousins lived on the same farm. Later, Clara would say that the years she spent there with her cousins were the happiest of her life.[13]

When Clara was eight her family sent her to a boarding school to help her overcome her shyness. It didn't work. She refused to eat and grew thin and pale. Years later, she claimed that she wasn't terribly homesick, just too shy to eat in front of the other children.[14] The school sent her home and her brothers and sisters took up her schooling again.

When Clara was about eleven, tragedy interrupted her lessons. David fell from the rafters at a barn raising and hit his head. For two years he was unable to get out of bed. Clara nursed him the entire time, rarely leaving his side. David eventually recovered completely. Caring for her brother gave Clara a boost in confidence.

Eventually Sarah got a turn to teach her youngest daughter. Later, Clara put her mother's cooking lessons to use on the battlefield many times.

Fortunately for Clara her parents allowed her to experience things most girls didn't during that era. Her brother taught her how to ride and throw a ball hard, like a boy. When they moved she spent an entire month learning how to hammer, saw, and paint. For a while she even worked in her family's cloth mill.

To her credit Clara found a role for herself. She tutored children in the community. Often she helped the poorer families. She was quick to volunteer during a smallpox epidemic and caught the disease herself. Her parents, both members of the Universalist Church, encouraged her charitable nature.

Still, Clara's sensitivity troubled her mother. She wasn't pleased with Clara's tomboyish ways either. Out of concern for Clara, Sarah turned to Lorenzo Niles Fowler, a phrenologist. At the time phrenology was an accepted science. It said that the bumps on a person's head determined their strengths and weaknesses. Years later Clara wrote of overhearing Mr. Fowler tell her mother that Clara should become a teacher: "The sensitive nature will always remain. She will never assert herself for herself; she will suffer wrong first. But for others she will be perfectly fearless. Throw responsibility upon her."[15]

It was the last thing Clara wanted to be, but her family persuaded her to become a teacher. They put her hair up and had a new green dress made for her. Later she wrote, "How well I remember the preparations—the efforts to look larger and older . . ."[16]

Sources vary on Clara's age when she started teaching. Some say she was as young as fifteen, others say seventeen. Later in life Clara kept meticulous diaries, but she was known to lie about her age. Early in her life, she said she was older. When she was older, she said she was younger. It's possible that she claimed she was seventeen to secure the job. Later Clara gave a hint as to her real age at this time: "Bright, rosy-cheeked boys and girls from four to thirteen, with the exception of four lads, as tall and nearly as old as myself."[17] It's doubtful that farm boys would still be in school at seventeen.

Despite her sensitive nature she took quick charge of the classroom and within a few days won the respect and admiration of her students. She made a strong impression on the four oldest boys when she stepped into their ballgame. "My four lads soon perceived that I was no stranger to their sports or their tricks. . . . When they found that I was as agile and as strong as themselves, that my throw was as sure and as straight as theirs, and that if they won a game it was because I permitted it, their respect knew no bounds."[18]

Clara's childhood and early adult years were similar to those of most New England girls born at the same time. However, it's easy to trace choices throughout her life back to those who influenced her the most: her soldier father, her strict mother, her sick brother, and even Dr. Fowler, who said she would be at her best helping others.

Deadly Smallpox

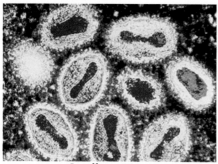
Smallpox Virus

For thousands of years, people have feared smallpox. It killed one out of three people who caught it. The first recorded smallpox epidemic was in 1350 BCE. By the fifth century CE, the disease had spread to Europe.

It is hard for people to prevent the disease because it spreads so easily. An infected person spews the virus into the air by coughing and sneezing. Anyone nearby is likely to breathe in the infected air. It isn't even necessary to be near an infected person. The virus can survive on blankets and clothing for a week.

An infected person gets sick about twelve days after they breathe in the virus. At first they have a high fever and a headache. They suffer from aches and pains all over their body. During this time the person can spread the disease to others, but often nobody knows the sickness is smallpox. When a rash appears a few days later, the disease is easy to diagnose. It's at this point that the patient is the most contagious. Eventually the rash turns into pus-filled blisters that scab over and fall off. These scabs often leave large scars.

In 1796 a doctor named Edward Jenner started working on a way to prevent smallpox. He had noticed that milkmaids who caught cowpox didn't catch smallpox. He took some fluid from a cowpox blister and injected it into a little boy. A few weeks later, he exposed the boy to smallpox. The boy never got sick with smallpox. Dr. Jenner used the word *vaccine,* which comes from the Latin word for cow, *vaca,* to describe his work.

Edward Jenner

At first people were afraid to be vaccinated, but the fear of smallpox was worse. Today there's still no treatment for smallpox. The best prevention is the vaccine.

Clara, at twenty-nine, was considered a spinster. She chose to teach rather than to marry.

CHAPTER
3

An Unmarried Woman

Clara's reputation for discipline and teaching reached other communities. For ten years, Clara taught at schools in North Oxford and the surrounding area. She would spend a term or two teaching order and respect to students at one school, and then move on to the next troubled school.

She once turned down a school in West Millbury when they offered her a reduced wage because she was a woman. "I may sometimes be willing to teach for nothing, but if paid at all, I shall never do a man's work for less than a man's pay," she told them. After they offered her the full salary, she stayed.[1]

Between 1845 and 1850 she helped her brother Stephen reform the schools in North Oxford. The community was a large mill town. Many of the mill workers' children didn't go to school. There was no school in the district where most of them lived. Clara and Stephen proposed a larger, newer school in the center of town, but many people were opposed because of the costs.

During a town meeting, a mill owner read a speech that Clara had written. Because she was a woman, she wasn't allowed to speak.[2] Stephen and Clara were successful. Just as the vote was to be taken, eighty-two factory and mill workers who were in favor of the school joined the meeting. Their votes made the difference.

Early in 1851, after a great deal of soul searching, Clara did the unexpected. She left teaching to attend school. At the time only a few schools admitted women. She chose the Clinton Liberal Institute in New York.

The college was coed, but women and men attended separate classes. She paid $35 a semester for tuition, room and board, and laundry. Perhaps hoping to blend in, she told no one how old she was or about her teaching experience. We don't know why but she didn't complete the course. Most likely she simply ran out of money.

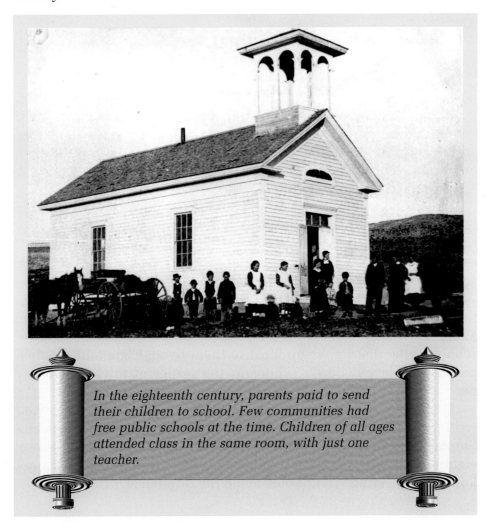

In the eighteenth century, parents paid to send their children to school. Few communities had free public schools at the time. Children of all ages attended class in the same room, with just one teacher.

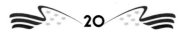

Clara returned home for a bit, but by the fall of 1851, she was teaching again, this time in Hightstown, New Jersey. She was bored and restless so she moved to Bordentown in 1852. Although New Jersey supported free public schools, they weren't successful. People avoided them because they thought of them as pauper schools.

It took a while but Clara persuaded the school board to let her open a free school. There were no students in the classroom that first morning, but a few boys sat on a rail fence outside. She met them cheerfully and then walked about the yard talking about birds and butterflies. When she finally went inside, six boys followed her. The next morning, twenty boys showed up for class. Nearly forty students were attending by the end of the week.[3] The school held only fifty students, but by the end of the second week, she had fifty-five. That fall, the school board opened a second free school.

To accommodate the increasing enrollment, the board built a new school large enough for six hundred children. The two-story brick school had eight classrooms, new desks, maps, and much more. Clara should have been happy but trouble was brewing. For one thing, religious groups demanded state money to open their own schools. Private schools closed because so many children were now attending Clara's school.

Worse, the school board decided to put a man in charge of her new school. They hired J. Kirby Burnham and made Clara his assistant. He earned $600 a year to her $250. Teachers were divided in their loyalty. Soon their quarrels made the newspaper. Clara couldn't take the pressure. She grew weak and lost her voice. Finally she resigned and left Bordentown in February 1854.

When the school board fired Burnham in May, Clara was recuperating in Washington, D.C. There she met Alexander DeWitt, a congressman from her home district in Massachusetts. Through him she met Charles Mason, who ran the Patent Office. In July 1854 Clara went to work for Mason, earning $1,400 a year.

Although there was no policy against employing women, most officials didn't. As far as Clara could tell, there were only four other female clerks in Washington. For his part Mason tried to protect Clara. During the six years she worked for the government, he never included her name in the official roll.[4]

Working in that office was difficult for Clara. She was the only woman there and the men were rude to her. They made catcalls, spit tobacco juice at her, and blew smoke in her face.[5] Washington society didn't approve of Clara's position in the office. Clara didn't care what anyone thought, which upset people even more. She was a wicked and scandalous woman in their eyes.

During this time Clara worked long hours at the office, suffered from bouts of malaria, and saved her money. Politics fascinated her and she spent her free time watching proceedings in the House and Senate. One evening in 1856 she listened to Senator Charles Sumner of Massachusetts deliver a speech against expanding slavery into the territories. The next day, Congressman Pierce Butler caught Sumner on the street and beat him. Clara realized that the country was seriously divided. "I have often said that that night war began! It began not at Sumter, but at Sumner," she told a friend years later.[6]

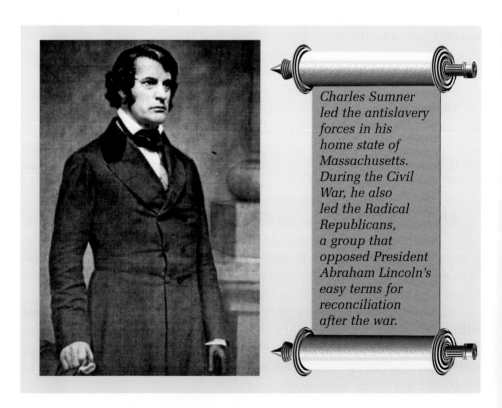

Charles Sumner led the antislavery forces in his home state of Massachusetts. During the Civil War, he also led the Radical Republicans, a group that opposed President Abraham Lincoln's easy terms for reconciliation after the war.

President Abraham Lincoln took office during troubled times. In fact, some historians believe his election actually triggered the Civil War.

Mason resigned in August 1857 and Clara was quickly fired. Relieved, she went home to North Oxford. What she had planned as a short visit lasted two years. Home wasn't very comforting. Captain Stephen and her favorite nephew, Irving, were sick. Relatives borrowed money from her. Throughout her life Clara's friends and family took advantage of her in this way. She seldom had the heart to refuse someone she loved. Once her savings were gone, she was a burden to her family. They wanted her to take a teaching position.

Unexpectedly the Patent Office recalled Clara. The country had elected Abraham Lincoln. The new president didn't mind women clerks. The Washington she returned to was more tense and rude than the one she had left. Everyone was waiting for war to break out between the North and South.

Clara was against slavery. She didn't think the South would remain estranged for long. At that time, she wrote about secession to her cousin Elvira Stone, "I believe the latter to be wearing out in its infancy and if wisely left alone will die a natural death, long before maturity."[7]

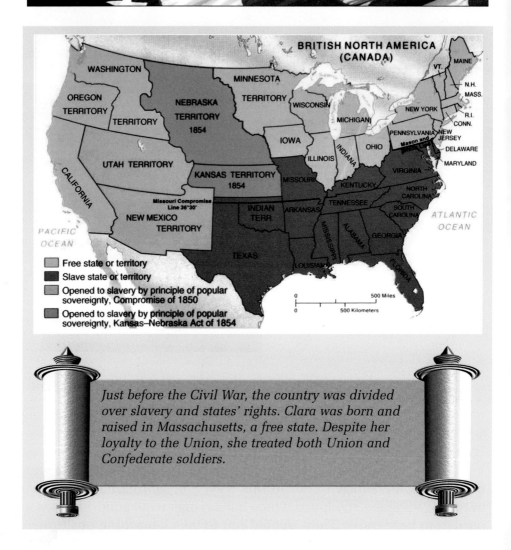

Just before the Civil War, the country was divided over slavery and states' rights. Clara was born and raised in Massachusetts, a free state. Despite her loyalty to the Union, she treated both Union and Confederate soldiers.

In March 1861 Clara sought the help of Senator Henry Wilson from Massachusetts. On the pretext of discussing the poor working conditions in the Patent Office, she secured an ally in her real cause—keeping her job even though she was a woman. Clara was safe, at least for a while. Little did she know that events beyond her control were about to change her life.

Clara's Views on Marriage

It wasn't unusual for young women to teach or to work in shops until they got married, but Clara never married. Stephen B. Oates said, "She hated all restrictions on women because of their sex and thought them entitled to the same rights as men. She had rejected marriage, which she associated with death, and had turned her back on the idea of marriage and mother-hood as the female ideal."[8] Elizabeth Brown Pryor doesn't agree. "Her disinclination to marry, at least during these early years, stemmed more from the unavailability of a suitable mate than from a strong prejudice against the subordinate role of women in marriage or a dislike of men,"[9] Pryor said. According to Clara's diaries and friends, she had a number of suitors.

Clara was well liked by men, and her family always insisted that she had plenty of suitors.[10] She told her cousin and biographer, William Barton, that "she chose, somewhat early in life, the course that seemed to her more fruitful of good for her than matrimony . . . she was so much interested in her school that she gave little thought to matrimony, and was satisfied that on the whole it would be better in her case if she lived unmarried. She had little patience, however, with women who affect to despise men . . . she was no man-hater, but on the contrary, enjoyed the society of men, trusted their judgment, and liked their companionship."[11]

In a letter to William Barton, Clara's nephew Stephen Barton provided the following: "She said that she had had her romances and love affairs like other girls; but that in her young womanhood, though she thought of different men as possible lovers, no one of them measured up to her ideal of a husband . . . she could think of herself with satisfaction as a wife and mother, but that on the whole . . . she had been more useful to the world by being free from matrimonial ties."[12] If we are to believe Clara's own words, she was happy with her status as a single woman.

Wedding gowns of the late 1800s

For Your Information

Citizens of Charleston, South Carolina, witness the Confederate attack on Fort Sumter in 1861.

CHAPTER
4

War!

On April 12, 1861, Southern rebels fired on Fort Sumter in South Carolina. There would be no peace between the North and South. The Sixth Massachusetts Regiment was one of the first to board a train for Washington, D.C. On April 19, they arrived in Baltimore, which in large part sympathized with the South.

In Baltimore the regiment marched through the streets for about a mile to catch another train. They expected trouble, but hoped for the best. From their shops and the streets, the people of Baltimore hollered angry curses and shook their fists at the soldiers. The first casualties of the American Civil War were in Baltimore that day. An angry mob killed three and wounded thirty. The soldiers ran for their lives and barely made it to the station to board a train for Washington. Through their coach windows, the soldiers watched the mob chase their train for several yards as it pulled out of the station.

In Washington, citizens gathered at the depot after hearing the news. Clara took the most seriously wounded to the home of her now-married sister Sally Vassal. The others camped out in the Capitol building. From those men, Clara learned that the Baltimore mob had seized their luggage. The men had no clothing or food. The next day, Clara persuaded grocers to donate food and other necessities. Clara had begun her service to the troops.

In July the grim reality of war showed itself when hundreds of wounded poured into Washington. They arrived tired, hungry, and dirty. Clara tended the wounded from a battle near Manassas, Virginia, that later became known as the first battle of Bull Run. Many soldiers had received no medical care or food before or during the evacuation to Washington. Northerners responded generously when Clara asked for supplies for the wounded. She knew the men would have enormous needs that the army was unprepared to fill. She rented space in a warehouse and actively solicited donations, even tobacco and whiskey.[1]

In February 1862 Clara traveled to North Oxford to care for her sick father. They talked about the war and he offered advice. She confided to him that she hoped to go to the battlefield, but she worried whether doing so was proper. She was convinced that better care at the battlefield would save lives. Captain Stephen encouraged his daughter to follow her heart. In war there wasn't room for frivolous concerns of modesty. After he passed away, Clara buried her father and then returned to Washington to wait.

Around that time she visited Colonel Daniel H. Rucker. She wanted to take her supplies to the front but needed a pass to get through the army's lines. As she spoke to the colonel, Clara began to cry. She tearfully explained that she had three warehouses full of food and hospital supplies. Rucker was moved. He not only gave Clara a pass, he gave her wagons in which to transport the goods, teamsters to drive the wagons, and men to load them. Biographers claim that Clara didn't cry from frustration or feminine weakness. She used tears to let the colonel know how strongly she felt about going to the battlefield.[2]

Clara was no longer working for the Patent Office, although she was still on the payroll and collecting half her wages. The office paid a substitute to work under her name so that Clara could tend to the wounded.

When Clara learned of the two thousand Union casualties at Cedar Mountain (also known as Cedar Run and Culpeper), she rounded up supplies and volunteers. They arrived on August 13, four days after the battle's end.

She found the wounded lying in their own blood and filth on the bare floors of private homes (the Main Street hospital was full). Their

The battle of Cedar Mountain was a Confederate victory. Had the troops not stopped to rest, they could have easily taken the Union capital at Washington, D.C.

wounds were severe—many had lost arms and legs. Some had lost part of their face or a hand or foot. They suffered from sunstroke, dehydration, and shock. She cooked, made bandages, talked with the wounded, and sometimes helped the surgeons. She even distributed goods to a group of wounded Confederate prisoners.

On August 30 during a routine trip to the hospital at Armory Square, she heard about the second battle of Bull Run near Manassas, Virginia. She requisitioned supplies from Colonel Rucker and the Sanitary Commission, a northern relief agency. The next morning she wrote a quick letter to her brother: "I leave immediately for the Battlefield . . . don't know when I can return. If anything happens [to]

The North and South met twice near Manassas, Virginia, near a stream named Bull Run. Both battles were Confederate victories. Casualties on both sides were high.

me you David must come and take all my effects home with you and Julia will know how to dispose of them."[3]

After traveling all night in a boxcar filled with supplies, Clara saw the hills where the battle had taken place. Wounded men covered the landscape in every direction.[4] Surrounded by their cries, Clara almost panicked.[5] Moments later she was serving hot food in empty canning jars.

During the early years of the war, Clara watched too many of the wounded die. Nearly 90 percent of those suffering a wound to the abdomen died, and 62 percent of the soldiers who received any other type of wound died.[6]

No stranger to hard work, Clara pinned her skirt up around her waist and got busy. From Bull Run to Harpers Ferry, her face stained with gunpowder, she comforted the wounded. She was almost always in danger of being hurt or even killed. Once she very nearly was killed when a bullet tore through the sleeve of her dress and hit a man she was tending to, killing him almost instantly. When a young soldier refused care, Clara discovered the boy was actually a young woman by the name of Mary Galloway.

After six weeks of following and tending to the wounded, Clara returned to Washington. She was sick with a fever and suffering from exhaustion. By October she had recuperated and rejoined the army at Harpers Ferry. As usual, a string of wagons loaded with supplies clattered along the trails with her. She traveled with the army as the

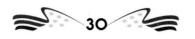

troops marched through the mountains of Virginia. In December 1862 she was with the Union troops at Fredericksburg, Virginia. By this time the army had a system for delivering the wounded to makeshift hospitals, but taking care of them was a different matter.

The army stuffed more than twelve hundred wounded troops into one house, the Lacy House, although official reports said only three hundred had been placed there.[7] Years later, Clara recalled the horror: "I wrung the blood from the bottom of my clothing, before I could step, for the weight about my feet."[8] She never forgot the suffering she saw in the Lacy House.

During the winter of 1863, Clara lobbied for improvements and more supplies. The army listened and made changes, making the Sanitary Commission its official civilian relief agency. When Clara asked for direct access to the army's stores, they refused her request. The very improvements she lobbied for blocked her efforts.

It was common for the troops to turn large homes, such as the Lacy House in Fredericksburg, Virginia, into makeshift hospitals. Often, these hospitals offered nothing more than a spot under a roof to die.

Commission directors and nurses kept her from ever serving under fire on the battlefield again.

For most of 1863 she worked with her brother David as a quartermaster in South Carolina. At Morris Island she demanded food and supplies for the wounded. Instead of appreciating her help, the professional army nurses and administrators resented her. They saw her demands as criticisms of their methods.[9] The army took her tent, hoping she would leave. Eventually General Gillmore, via a short note, insisted she leave.

The qualities that had made Clara indispensable early in the war now made her a target. Clara worked well alone. The relief efforts had become organized, and she found it difficult to work with others. In short, she annoyed people and refused to work within the new system.

When the carnage of Spotsylvania, Virginia, overwhelmed the Sanitary Commission, the secretary of war gave Clara a pass to join the forces there. Rain was the real enemy. Wounded soldiers died of exposure and shock when ambulances sat stuck in the mud for days. Clara was horrified to learn that Union officers refused to ask the Southern-sympathizing citizens of Fredericksburg to provide food and supplies for the Union's wounded soldiers. She complained to Senator Wilson in Washington, and by the next morning, Fredericksburg's citizens opened their homes to the "dirty, lousy soldiers" of the Union army.[10]

In June of 1864, General Benjamin Butler put her in charge of nursing at the Tenth Army Corps Hospital near Point of Rocks, Virginia. Most of the men suffered from disease rather than battle wounds. In this position, Clara worked under military authority. She was no longer a volunteer.

When Butler was relieved for incompetence, Clara returned to Washington in January 1865. For four years, she had championed the war's wounded and sick as an advocate and nurse.

The war was all but over, but Clara certainly wasn't finished.

Mary Galloway, Soldier in Love

Battle of Antietam

The fall of 1861 was a bad time to fall in love, but that's exactly what Mary Galloway and Lieutenant Harry Barnard did. When his regiment left for South Mountain and Antietam, Mary was inconsolable. She donned a Union uniform and tried to follow, claiming to be the hospital steward. She was barely sixteen. Mary was slender and wore her hair cut short. In her uniform she easily passed for a young man.[11]

A bullet struck Mary in the neck during the Battle of Antietam on September 17, 1862. She lay in a ditch for a day and a half. Mary refused to let the surgeons attend her, and they sought out Clara.

The bullet had passed almost all the way through her neck. The surgeon slit her flesh and removed the bullet. Clara looked after Mary until she was well. Mary returned home without seeing Harry or learning any news of him.

Late in October, Clara found Harry among the wounded at a hospital in Frederick, Maryland. He was struggling in fear with a nurse and two surgeons who were trying to amputate his gangrenous arm. Harry, delirious with fever and pain, cried out for Mary.

Clara knew exactly what to do. She told Harry that she would find Mary and bring her to him. Only then would he agree to allow the surgeons to do whatever they needed to do. It just so happened that Mary was from Frederick, and it didn't take long for Clara to find her. The brave girl held her beloved Harry's hand until he fell asleep. While he was unconscious, the surgeons sawed off his blackened arm.

Amputation Saw

After the Civil War, Clara continued to help people by searching for missing solders. She also spoke out for women's rights and an end to slavery. In 1881, she became the first president of the American Red Cross.

CHAPTER
5

The American Red Cross Is Born

With Senator Wilson's help, Clara won President Lincoln's approval to work with released prisoners of war at Annapolis. The War Department had no idea how to use Clara—despite Lincoln's expressed desire that they do so. With little else to do, Clara began compiling information about dead and missing Union soldiers. Her first list of missing had twenty thousand names. She received no pay for her work.

That summer, Clara met Dorence Atwater. He had spent two years as a prisoner at Andersonville Prison. At the prison hospital, he had recorded the name, rank, and cause of death for each prisoner who died. He made a second list, which he kept a secret. That summer, he and Clara traveled to Andersonville, Georgia. Day after day, they matched the numeric grave markers to the names on Atwater's list. When they were done, thirteen thousand graves were properly marked using the soldiers' names—they were meaningless numbers no more. Only about four hundred were marked "Unknown U.S. Soldier."[1] When they dedicated the new cemetery on August 17, Clara was proud to be the one raising the United States flag over the prison.

Clara returned to Washington, D.C., and continued her mission to find missing soldiers. In November, the Patent Office removed her from the payroll permanently. Suddenly Clara had no income. As happened so often in her life, she felt abused and forgotten.[2]

About this time, an old friend turned up and changed Clara's life. While nursing in South Carolina, Clara had met Frances Gage, a feminist. They became good friends. Aunt Fanny, as Clara called her, encouraged Clara to try public speaking. It was a way Clara could publicize her work and earn a living. Together they also presented a petition to Congress for $15,000 to continue her work on the missing-soldiers project. Of that, $12,000 was to reimburse Clara for the money she'd spent during the war. The remaining $3,000 would cover the cost of Clara's correspondence with missing men and their families.[3]

Clara never proved whether she actually spent $12,000 of her own money during the war. She kept no receipts or records. Her salary from the Patent Office was about $700 a year. Furthermore, she had no substantial savings before the war. How she determined the figure $12,000, we'll never know. A traditional story says that a suitor from North Oxford made a fortune in California during the Gold Rush in 1849. She refused to marry him, but he sent her $10,000 just the same. She spent it during the Civil War.[4]

Even without documentation of Clara's expenses, Congress granted the petition. She used some of the grant money to hire clerks and outfit the Office of Correspondence with Friends of the Missing Men of the United States Army.

In the fall of 1866, Clara traveled through New England delivering her first lecture, "Work and Incidents of Army Life." Despite her stage fright, she was a good speaker. She was also a popular speaker, and she charged the same fee as a male lecturer, $75 to $100 per lecture.[5]

If she hadn't been a feminist before the war, she certainly was one afterward. The war had changed everything for women, according to Clara: "Only an opportunity was wanting for women to prove to man that she could be in earnest—that she had character, and firmness of purpose. . . . The war afforded her this opportunity."[6]

For the remainder of her life, Clara supported women's rights, but she did so quietly. The right of women to vote was never her main objective. Clara was more interested in helping the freed slaves assimilate into society. She spoke about this in 1868: "No person in this house could be more rejoiced than myself if it could be decided to admit at the same moment to a voice in the Government all persons and classes naturally and properly entitled to it . . . But if the door be not wide enough to admit us all at once—and one must wait—then I am willing. I am willing to stand back and see the old, scared limping slave clank his broken fetters through before me—while I stand back with head uncovered—thanking God for his release."[7]

Meanwhile the lecture circuit took its toll on Clara's health. In spring 1868 she lost her voice—an all too familiar symptom by this time. A year later she was still too weak to return to public speaking. Her doctor in North Oxford recommended she take a trip to Europe. Clara closed the Office of Correspondence with Friends of the Missing Men of the United States Army. The office had received and answered 63,182 letters and identified 22,000 men.

In Geneva, Switzerland, Clara met Dr. Louis Appia, a member of the International Red Cross. Clara was surprised to learn that the United States government wasn't participating in the organization. Before Clara could return home, war broke out between France and Prussia (Germany). In Switzerland, Clara made bandages for the Red Cross and came face to face with the impact of war on civilians. She saw the homeless women and children wandering the streets and begging for food. She worried about the displaced women and children she saw as they traveled through the ruined villages.

Clara knew it would take more than charity to rebuild their broken lives. They needed to work. She and Grand Duchess Louise of Baden opened a sewing room. Women picked up fabric and supplies with which to make clothing. The organization paid these women a small wage when they returned a finished garment. Then Clara's organization distributed the new clothes to war victims. The women earned a living and contributed to their community. It was a huge success, employing three hundred women at one point.

For her work, the emperor and empress of Germany awarded Barton the Iron Cross of Merit. She also received the Gold Cross of Remembrance from the grand duke and duchess of Baden.

After three years of touring Europe and helping in the war relief efforts, Clara returned to the United States. Despite her accomplishments, she was exhausted and depressed. She suffered her worst emotional breakdown and spent most of the next two years in bed, unable to see, talk, or even move.

In March 1876 Clara entered Our Home on the Hillside, a health center in Dansville, New York. The center emphasized a healthy diet, plenty of fresh air, and exercise. There, Clara grew stronger. She adopted many of the lifestyle changes she learned at the center. She never again suffered from a serious emotional breakdown.

Once Clara recovered, she wrote to Dr. Appia in Switzerland about starting an American Red Cross Society. The International Red Cross in Europe made Clara its representative to Washington. For better or worse, getting the United States to accept the Red Cross was the biggest battle of Clara's life. No one was interested. The country was at peace and people saw no need for a war relief organization. Besides, most politicians were leery of joining an international society. Other countries might take advantage of their membership in the organization to interfere with the United States government and its policies.

In response Clara wrote a small pamphlet, titled "The Red Cross of the Geneva Convention: What It Is." She explained that the Red Cross provided guidelines for the fair and humane treatment of war prisoners and protected medical personnel. She even met with the president, Rutherford B. Hayes, but got nowhere. She continued her campaign and used her own money to promote the cause.

When forest fires destroyed thousands of homes in Michigan, Clara raised $80,000. She sent medicine, clothing, and tools to the devastated areas. The new president, Chester Arthur, noticed Clara's work with the agency. He was so impressed with the agency's work that he signed the Treaty of Geneva on March 1, 1882. Clara appeared before the Senate Foreign Relations Committee on the treaty's behalf. On March 16, 1882, the Senate ratified the Treaty of Geneva, also known as the Geneva Convention. However, the American Red Cross didn't receive its first congressional charter until 1900. This charter, which remains in effect today, allows the Red Cross to communicate with people in the armed forces and their families in an official capacity. For instance, the Red Cross contacts servicemen who are serving overseas when there has been a death in the family or when a baby is born. Until the charter was granted, the American Red Cross was really a disaster relief fund. Now the Red Cross also works with the government on behalf of servicemen.

It was only natural that the new American Red Cross Society unanimously elected Clara its first president. In September 1884, she traveled to Geneva to attend the Third International Conference of the Red Cross. She was proud to be the first woman to

In May of 1889, 2,209 people died in a tremendous flood that devastated Johnstown, Pennsylvania. Clara, sixty-seven, arrived with five Red Cross workers five days later. It was the agency's first peacetime relief effort.

officially represent the United States government at an international conference.

Clara dedicated herself completely to the American Red Cross for the next twenty years. Under her leadership, the American Red Cross lent aid all over the country: to flood victims in Pennsylvania; to tornado survivors in Alabama and Louisiana; to earthquake survivors in Charleston, South Carolina; to drought victims in Texas; to those who suffered during a yellow fever epidemic in Florida; and more. Branches of the Red Cross opened around the country.

In 1893 Clara traveled to Asia on behalf of the Red Cross when Turkish soldiers attacked Armenian villages. She was seventy-seven when she sailed to Cuba with supplies during the Spanish-American War. Tradition tells us that Theodore Roosevelt, then a colonel in the army, tried to buy supplies for his men from Clara. She told him her supplies weren't for sale, but that the Red Cross would freely supply whatever he needed. The Pasha of Constantinople awarded Clara the Second Order of Shefafet for her service. She was the first woman to receive the honor.

In 1893, a hurricane destroyed Morris Island, South Carolina, killing hundreds of people there. Clara led a Red Cross relief effort to help survivors. Thirty years earlier, she had nursed Union soldiers in the same city.

Eventually Clara's enthusiasm waned. She had never been fond of sharing responsibility or the limelight, and this didn't change as she aged. Nor was she open to anyone's ideas but her own. Clara didn't want interference from anyone. She ran the Red Cross as she pleased, just as she had taken charge on the battlefield. She was bossy and stubborn and lots of people didn't like her. Some even went so far as to accuse her of mishandling Red Cross funds.

Clara never abused her position or wasted the society's money. She simply failed to keep good records and receipts. Had she cooperated with others, they probably would have been more

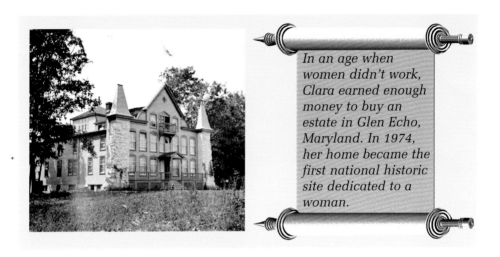

In an age when women didn't work, Clara earned enough money to buy an estate in Glen Echo, Maryland. In 1974, her home became the first national historic site dedicated to a woman.

accepting of her disorganized methods. The truth is that she rubbed people the wrong way. In 1904 at the age of eighty-three, Clara resigned her position with the Red Cross. She retired to her home in Glen Echo, Maryland.

She continued to speak and traveled to Russia to attend a Red Cross conference. While there, Czar Nicholas II awarded her the Silver Cross of Imperial Russia. She wrote a few books, including *The Story of My Childhood.* She remained active, cooking and cleaning for herself. She milked her cow, raked leaves, and tended her garden. Many people claimed that she gardened while wearing her many awards pinned to her chest.

On the morning of April 12, 1912, Clara opened her eyes and said, "Let me go, let me go," just before she died. She was ninety years old and had been ill for several months.

Clara was born into a time when a woman's expectations were limited. As a teacher, she inspired her students. During the Civil War, she comforted and assisted in the evacuation of thousands of wounded soldiers. She overcame fear and depression to become one of the most beloved heroines in United States history. In truth, she was respected and loved throughout the western world, not just in the United States. Thanks to Clara's persistence and hard work, the American Red Cross is the largest humanitarian organization in the United States. Millions of people owe their lives to the relief efforts of the American Red Cross and its tireless and committed founder, Clara Barton.

Andersonville Prison

Early in the war, the United States government refused to exchange prisoners with the Confederates. Then in 1862 the two governments finally came to terms: sixty enlisted men for one general, fifteen enlisted for a colonel, four enlisted for a lieutenant, and two enlisted for a sergeant. When General Ulysses S. Grant became commander of the Union Army, he stopped the exchange process.

When the Union prisoners outgrew the facility at Richmond, Virginia, the Confederates built a fort early in 1864 near Andersonville, Georgia. Later the fort became known as Andersonville Prison. They chose the site because it had a water source and was near a railroad.

The original camp was a simple stockade of pine logs. The enclosure was over sixteen acres. They planned to confine as many as ten thousand prisoners. Within months of opening, over thirty-two thousand prisoners were crammed into the camp.

During the fourteen months that the camp existed, almost fifty thousand Union soldiers passed through its gates. Every thirty yards a guard kept watch over the wall and the enclosure. A small stream flowed through the middle of the enclosure. There was a second wall, called the deadline, inside the outer stockade. Sentries shot any prisoner caught between the two walls.

The Confederacy didn't provide enough food, and many prisoners died of starvation. In the overcrowded conditions, the stream was soon polluted. Thirteen thousand died from disease, malnutrition, and exposure in a little over a year.

Eventually, the United States charged General Robert E. Lee and several other Confederate generals and politicians with conspiring to injure or kill prisoners. President Andrew Johnson dropped the charges in August 1865 against everyone but Henry Wirz, the camp's commander. A military commission found Wirz guilty, and he was hanged on November 10. He claimed to the end that he wasn't guilty. Throughout the execution, Union soldiers chanted, "Wirz, remember, Andersonville."

Chapter Notes

Chapter 1 Angel of the Battlefield

1. William E. Barton, *The Life of Clara Barton: Founder of the American Red Cross,* Vol. 1 (Boston: Houghton Mifflin Company, 1922), p. 175.
2. Stephen B. Oates, *A Woman of Valor: Clara Barton and the Civil War* (New York: The Free Press, 1994), p. 14.
3. Ibid., p. 68.
4. Ibid., p. 69.
5. Barton, p. 177.
6. Ibid., p. 178.
7. Ishbel Ross, *Angel of the Battlefield: The Life of Clara Barton* (New York: Harper & Brothers Publishers, 1956), p. 34.
8. Oates, p. 70.
9. Barton, p. 181.
10. Ibid., p. 189.

Chapter 2 From Tot to Teacher

1. Elizabeth Brown Pryor, *Clara Barton: Professional Angel* (Philadelphia: University of Pennsylvania Press, 1987), p. 3.
2. William E. Barton, *The Life of Clara Barton: Founder of the American Red Cross,* Vol. 1 (Boston: Houghton Mifflin Company, 1922), p. 17.
3. Pryor, p. 3.
4. Barton, p. 8.
5. Ibid., p. 19.
6. Ibid., pp. 19–20.
7. Pryor, p. 7.
8. Barton, p. 18.
9. Pryor, p. 11.
10. Barton, p. 20.
11. Ibid., p. 22.
12. Ibid., p. 131.
13. Pryor, p. 14.
14. Barton, p. 29.
15. Ishbel Ross, *Angel of the Battlefield: The Life of Clara Barton* (New York: Harper & Brothers Publishers, 1956), p. 11.
16. Barton, p. 51.
17. Ibid., p. 51.
18. Ibid., p. 52.

Chapter 3 An Unmarried Woman

1. Elizabeth Brown Pryor, *Clara Barton: Professional Angel* (Philadelphia: University of Pennsylvania Press, 1987), p. 23.
2. Ibid., p. 29.
3. Ibid., p. 49.
4. Ibid., p. 57.
5. Ibid., p. 61.
6. Ibid., p. 63.
7. Ibid., p. 74.
8. Stephen B. Oates, *A Woman of Valor: Clara Barton and the Civil War* (New York: The Free Press, 1994), p. 7.
9. Pryor, p. 27.
10. Ishbel Ross, *Angel of the Battlefield: The Life of Clara Barton* (New York: Harper & Brothers Publishers, 1956), p. 17.
11. William E. Barton, *The Life of Clara Barton: Founder of the American Red Cross* (Cambridge, Massachusetts: Houghton Mifflin Company, 1922), pp. 76–77.
12. Ibid., p. 77.

Chapter 4 War!

1. Elizabeth Brown Pryor, *Clara Barton: Professional Angel* (Philadelphia: University of Pennsylvania Press, 1987), p. 81.
2. Ibid., p. 88.
3. Ibid., p. 92.
4. Ibid., p. 92.
5. Ibid., p. 93.
6. Ibid., p. 94.
7. Ibid., p. 107.
8. Ibid., p. 107.
9. Ibid., p. 118.
10. Ibid., p. 126.
11. Stephen B. Oates, *A Woman of Valor: Clara Barton and the Civil War* (New York: The Free Press, 1994), p. 91.

Chapter 5 The American Red Cross Is Born

1. Elizabeth Brown Pryor, *Clara Barton: Professional Angel* (Philadelphia: University of Pennsylvania Press, 1987), p. 140.
2. Ibid., pp. 145–146.
3. Ibid., p. 146.
4. Ishbel Ross, *Angel of the Battlefield: The Life of Clara Barton* (New York: Harper & Brothers Publishers, 1956), p. 17.
5. Pryor, p. 149.
6. Ibid., p. 151.
7. Ibid., p. 153.

Chronology

1821	Clarissa Harlowe Barton is born on December 25 in North Oxford, Massachusetts.
1825	She begins school at the age of four.
1833–35	Clara cares for her brother David after he sustains a serious head injury.
1839	A young Miss Barton begins her career as a teacher.
1845	Clara establishes a free public school for the children of mill workers in North Oxford.
1846	Her sister Dorothea "Dolly" Barton dies after a long bout with mental illness.
1851	Clara attends the Clinton Liberal Institute in New York. Her mother, Sarah Barton, dies.
1852	Clara establishes New Jersey's first free public school.
1854	She moves to Washington, D.C., and takes a job as a clerk in the U.S. Patent Office.
1861	Clara begins volunteer work as a nurse to Union soldiers in Washington, D.C.
1862	She receives a pass to nurse soldiers on the battlefield. Her father, Captain Stephen Barton, dies.
1863	Clara travels to Hilton Head, South Carolina.
1864	She returns to Washington, D.C., and takes charge of nursing at a field hospital.
1865–68	Clara finds and identifies more than 22,000 missing or dead soldiers from the Civil War. During this time, she helps establish Andersonville National Cemetery in Georgia.
1866–68	She is paid to give more than 200 lectures on her experiences in the Civil War.
1869	Clara travels to Europe to recuperate from illness. There she meets Dr. Appia and learns about the International Red Cross.
1870–71	She takes part in Red Cross relief efforts during the Franco-Prussian War.
1873	Clara receives the Iron Cross of Merit from the emperor of Germany. She returns to the United States, where she suffers a nervous breakdown. It takes two years for her to recover.
1875	She begins her campaign to establish a Red Cross chapter in the United States.
1881	Clara leads the country's first chapter of the American Red Cross, in Dansville, New York. She becomes the organization's first president.
1884	Clara represents the United States at the Third International Conference of the Red Cross in Geneva, Switzerland. She becomes the first woman to represent the United States in a foreign country.
1896	She travels to Turkey to take part in relief efforts after the Armenian massacres.
1898	At the age of 77, Clara Barton publishes *The Red Cross: A History*.
1900	After a devastating hurricane, Clara travels to Galveston, Texas, with the Red Cross.
1904	She resigns as president of the American Red Cross.
1912	Clara dies at her home in Glen Echo, Maryland, on April 12.

Timeline in History

1776   Representatives of the thirteen American colonies declare their independence from England, starting the Revolutionary War.

1781   Articles of Confederation are adopted by the new United States government. Cornwallis surrenders at Yorktown, ending the Revolutionary War.

1789   The United States Constitution is ratified. George Washington becomes the first president of the United States. Thomas Jefferson witnesses the fall of the Bastille and the opening events of the French Revolution.

1804–06 Lewis and Clark travel across the continent to the Pacific Ocean.

1852   Harriet Beecher Stowe publishes *Uncle Tom's Cabin.*

1860   South Carolina secedes from the Union. Mississippi, Florida, Alabama, Georgia, Louisiana, and Texas follow soon after.

1861   The American Civil War begins on April 12 when Confederate soldiers fire on Fort Sumter.

1863   The International Red Cross is founded in Geneva, Switzerland.

1864   The first Geneva Convention adopts rules for protecting sick and wounded on the battlefield.

1865   The American Civil War ends.

1870   The Fifteenth Amendment to the Constitution, giving blacks the right to vote, is ratified.

1870–71 Franco-Prussian War is fought.

1882   President Chester A. Arthur signs the Treaty of Geneva. America joins the International Committee of the Red Cross.

1895   Cuban Revolution is fought.

1898   American Red Cross provides service for military forces for the first time as Spanish-American War begins.

1903   The Wright Brothers make their first sustained flight in Kitty Hawk, North Carolina.

1910   Henry Dunant, the founder of the Red Cross in Europe, dies.

1914–18 United States enters World War I.

1919   The Nineteenth Amendment to the Constitution, giving women the right to vote, is ratified.

1932   Hattie Wyatt Caraway is the first woman elected to the U.S. Senate (filling the vacancy left by her husband's death). Amelia Earhart completes the first solo nonstop transatlantic flight by a woman.

1941   U.S. declares war on Japan after Japan attacks Pearl Harbor in Hawaii.

1945   The United Nations is established.

Further Reading

For Young Adults

Collier, James Lincoln. *The Clara Barton You Never Knew.* Danbury, Connecticut: Children's Press, 2004.

Ditchfield, Christin. *Clara Barton: Founder of the American Red Cross.* New York: Franklin Watts, 2004.

Francis, Dorothy. *Clara Barton: Founder of the American Red Cross.* Brookfield, Connecticut: The Millbrook Press, 2002.

Klingel, Cynthia, and Robert B. Noyed. *Clara Barton: Founder of the American Red Cross.* Chanhassen, Minnesota: The Child's World, 2003.

Somervill, Barbara A. *Clara Barton: Founder of the American Red Cross.* Minneapolis, Minnesota: Compass Point Books, 2007.

Works Consulted

Barton, William E. *The Life of Clara Barton: Founder of the American Red Cross.* Volumes 1 and 2. Boston: Houghton Mifflin Company, 1922.

Epler, Percy Harold. *The Life of Clara Barton.* New York: The MacMillan Company, 1938.

Hutchinson, John F. *Champions of Charity: War and the Rise of the Red Cross.* Boulder, Colorado: Westview Press, 1996.

Oates, Stephen B. *A Woman of Valor: Clara Barton and the Civil War.* New York: The Free Press, 1994.

Oates, Stephen B. *The Approaching Fury: Voices of the Storm, 1820–1861.* New York: HarperCollins Publishers, 1997.

Pryor, Elizabeth Brown. *Clara Barton: Professional Angel.* Philadelphia: University of Pennsylvania Press, 1987.

Ross, Ishbel. *Angel of the Battlefield: The Life of Clara Barton.* New York: Harper & Brothers Publishers, 1956.

On the Internet

American Red Cross
  www.redcross.org

Civil War Medicine
  http://www.civilwarhome.com/civilwarmedicineintro.htm

Clara Barton, 1821–1912, Civil War Nurse, Founder American Red Cross
  http://www.americancivilwar.com/women/cb.html

Clara Barton Chronology 1821–1860
  http://www.nps.gov/archive/clba/chron1.html

The Federal Charter of the American Red Cross
  http://mowercounty.redcross.org/AboutUs/charters2.html

Geocities: Life Stories or Civil War Heroes, Index to Clara Barton's Pages
  http://www.geocities.com/Athens/Aegean/6732/cb.html

Historic Medical Sites in the Washington, D.C., Area by Inci A. Bowman, Ph.D.
  http://www.nlm.nih.gov/hmd/medtour/intro.html

National Museum of Civil War Medicine
  http://www.civilwarmed.org/

Glossary

amputate (AM-pyoo-tayt)
To surgically remove.

artillery (ar-TIL-uh-ree)
Big guns, such as cannons, used on the battlefield.

cavalry (KAH-vul-ree)
Special military unit that uses horses.

civilian (sih-VIL-yun)
A person who is not on active duty in a military unit.

Confederacy (kun-FEH-duh-ruh-see)
The union of the southern states, which seceded (withdrew) from the United States during the Civil War.

evacuate (ee-VAH-kyoo-ayt)
To move people from a dangerous place to a safe place.

gangrenous (GANG-gruh-nus)
Having gangrene, a condition in which the tissue has died, and as it decays, it causes infection.

quartermaster (KWAR-ter-mas-ter)
A military officer who provides shelter, clothing, fuel, and other living arrangements for the troops.

Union (YOON-yun)
Another name for the United States, it usually refers to the federal troops during the Civil War.

Index